HEALING ELLIE
HEALING ME

HEALING ELLIE
HEALING ME
A True Story

Cindi McGrath

An Inspire-Ink Press Book

INSPIREINK

For Luke

For teaching me that every life's journey is
its own, is sacred.

For Ellie

Who, while I was suffering with the
question "WHY is this dog in my life?"
placed a very large paw in my hand, looked
deep into my eyes, and said to me, pleaded
with me,
'Help me. You show me how to heal. I
don't know another way. I don't want
to be a bad dog.'

Forthcoming by Cindi McGrath

Non-Fiction Prose
I Don't Remember
Audio or PDF Download
Available January 2017

Healing Ellie Healing Me
Audiobook CD
Narrated by the Author
Available April 2017

365 Mornings
Poetry

Kato! A Frog on a Dog in a Bog
Illustrated Children's Book
For Ages 3 to 103

Angel in a Purple Sweater
Poetry

Acknowledgments

I would like to express my gratitude to the many people and animals who saw me through this book from the very night Ellie found me to the present, sharing Ellie's story with all who may find this book in their hands.

Thank you to Daphne Michaels, Nancy Rebecca, Yvonne Kilcup, Asia Voight, Shannon Harder Ronald, Maura Cashman Nelson, and Allison Slavick for your guidance, teachings, friendship, seemingly endless knowledge, and for continually challenging me to evolve, expand, and "Write, write, write!"

Thank you, Christopher Schmidt, for the inspired and brilliant cover design, and for patiently and quickly responding to my many requests for additions, deletions, edits, and 'just one more thing.'

Thank you, Shellie Milford, for your editing in the final hours before this book went to print; spending time during your Christmas holiday reading, editing, reading again, offering your comments and suggestions, correcting my grammatical errors, and sharing many pet stories of your own.

Thank you, Cynthia Samels, for caring as deeply as I do for the dogs of the world, and for lifting my spirits when we learned that our little terriers, Mufasa and Willie, were not able to be saved from the past traumas they endured at the hands of humans.

Thank you to The Dog; to dogs unknown, and to the dogs with which I have shared this life. Thank you, Tasha, for teaching me the language of the dog when I was but a toddler. And thank you to the dogs of more recent years: Joey, Jack, Luke, Olive, Kato, and Ellie, for your companionship, for giving me a reason to laugh out loud, and for the tears I have shed upon you and for you.

And my deepest, heartfelt gratitude to my husband, Chris. Thank you from the depths of my soul for your patience and unwavering support of my work. For cooking my meals, entertaining our dogs, and keeping our house in order while I finished this book, I am eternally grateful. It brings me joy to be walking with you in this life.

Ellie

Contents

HEALING ELLIE
HEALING ME

Introduction

I wasn't looking for another dog. There were three Labradors in our home and not a week had passed since losing our beloved dog, Luke. That's not exactly right; let me restate that. Not a week had passed since Luke's life was taken from him; taken from him on a day when, despite the disease that was consuming him, he was not ready to die. My heart would ache, will continue to ache for years, with grief and guilt at Luke's passing. No, I wasn't looking for another dog. I had also not yet recovered from the pain and anxiety of losing, and then being reunited with, our young Labrador Kato. Not lost as in runaway-dog lost; lost because I had signed a contract. Lost because I had made numerous decisions with my head and not my heart. But this is not Kato's story, although you will meet him in the pages that follow. This is Ellie's story. The dog I wasn't looking for. The dog who would cause me on more than one occasion to ask, often through sobbing tears and barely able to breathe, "Why is this dog in my life?"

The story that follows is the true story of Ellie's and my shared journey of self-discovery and healing. Ellie, abused and tortured before being cast aside as a not-quite-four-month-old puppy. This is her story of transformation. Discovered living in a culvert, starving and covered with wounds and parasites; this is Ellie's journey from a distrustful and traumatized puppy to a healthy, happy, 120-pound lapdog. That Ellie found the one person, *the only person,* who could save her was destiny. Animal communicator and intuitive healer I heard Ellie's plea for help, Why was I unlovable to them? Help me. YOU show me how to heal. I don't know another way. I don't want to be a bad dog.

Ellie's anxieties were many. Along the path of her recovery I was moved to ask, *What do you need from me, Ellie? Where do I even begin to help you through all of this trapped anger and rage? I want to help you, Ellie, but you need to help me understand. What does Ellie want?*

This story is not simply another story of the bad dog turned good dog. Unlike many stories told from a dog's perspective, Ellie's story is different. Ellie's story is true. A true tale of neglect, torture, and abuse followed by rescue, deep struggle, and healing. Ellie's journey toward healing began in October 2012 when she was discovered after having survived alone in a forest for many weeks. She was not yet twenty weeks old.

The dialogues that ensued over the following years document a shared journey of pain and progress. A dog that surely would have been abandoned yet again by most others, I heard Ellie, and I felt her pain. I committed myself to her recovery and devoted my energies to facilitating her healing.

Along with me, my husband Chris and our three Labradors guided Ellie along a difficult path of learning how to live with other beings, how to trust, and how to live life with joy. Ellie wishes for the story of her journey to touch millions of people, wishes for all dogs to know the love of humanity, and for no human or dog, for no one, to suffer as she has suffered.

ALONE

And then I...ummm...they were gone. And
then I was outside. Like totally outside.
There was no more inside. I had to wander
around, you know? I was by myself. Alone.
And I just wandered.   Wandered and
wandered and wandered and wandered and
wandered and wandered, wandered, wandered,
wandered, wandered, wandered...I think I must not
have been my correct weight. I must have
been pretty underweight. And then I went
someplace else; I wasn't here. I was actually
at one other place for a little bit of time.

Yes, Ellie, they threw you away and you were alone in the forest. Alone to wander and wander and wander. And you were very, very thin. Because you were so thin and had hundreds of ticks attached to you, the veterinarian said that you were probably alone and wandered for a month or more. You were barely four months old when they left you, Ellie. You are amazing for surviving not only what they did to you, but also for living alone in a forest near the wolves, coyotes, and bears for many weeks. And you are right; you did go to two different places before you came home to us.

A fall evening in late October. The evening Ellie found me. Less than a week had passed since we had said goodbye to our beloved Rottweiler, Luke. The paralyzing guilt I would feel over Luke's euthanasia would surface months later. Guilt over having a lethal injection take our beautiful Luke away on a day when, despite the crippling pain he suffered on most days, he was not in pain. Ending his life on a day when he was content, happy, and filled with love and joy. Ending his life because the appointment had been made. The veterinarian had arrived at our home in a rush, late and with car trouble at the end of his day. He wasn't our regular vet. He didn't know Luke. Chris had barely a moment to say goodbye; my heart closed tight to block out the pain. It was time because time in our world said it was time.

On this late October day, there was deep sadness in missing Luke. Walking with my Labrador Kato along a winding, wooded trail, daylight faded. The sky dark yet brilliant. Clouds of maroon, dark pink and red. Driving west out of the park gazing at the clouds, I wondered at the severity of the colors and how they merged with my sadness. *Are you up there, Luke? I'm so sorry, I miss you so much.*

I am brought quickly back to the present as a skinny black dog dashes out of a culvert, bores its eyes deep into mine, and retreats. *Oh boy, here we go.* I remember the thought clearly. Yes, here we go.

Thinking first of Kato, I park my truck and get his attention. "Hey, Kato. Wait here for me my good boy." He immediately settled into his blankets with a chew bone. At the culvert, I am greeted with a distrustful growl. Seeing how

7

thin this dog is I ignore the growl, start humming softly and sit in the leaf littered ditch. The culvert spanning the underside of the road is obviously home; there are chew marks on the edge, and the dog is guarding the entrance walking in tight circles. Watching, I can see this is a girl dog. "You're okay now girlie girl," I sing softly, inching a little closer. Head cocked with curiosity, but eyes narrowed in distrust, she backs into the culvert. Singing, humming, filling my heart with love, I wait. She crawls out on her belly and looks at me with head level, facial muscles taut with fear. I toss a leather lead loosely around her neck. She sits up quickly, eyeing me suspiciously. Gazing at her with love in my heart, I don't move.

Apparently satisfied with her visual examination, she lies down in the leaves, curls her body into a tight circle and falls instantly asleep. I now see how thin she is, and there is a tight collar around her neck. *Puppy?* I wonder. As thin as she is she is a big dog, perhaps fifty-five pounds. That she might be a puppy hadn't crossed my mind, yet the collar appears to be boring into the skin of her neck. Slowly, I move toward the dog and am now sitting next to her. She opens one eye for a moment, then back to sleep. I softly stroke the top of her head and she releases a long, mournful sigh. There are ticks too numerous to count covering her head. Ticks and scabs and small lesions cover every inch of her body. Every rib is prominent, her spine and hip bones clearly visible; yet wearing a collar that is digging into her skin. *Someone must be missing this puppy,* I foolishly think. Without thinking, rather, without feeling, I call the sheriff to report a missing puppy. As I listen to the phone ring I allow my mind to overrule my heart; a puppy hiding in a ditch and wearing a collar must certainly be lost. Thirty minutes pass before an arrogant, insensitive city police officer arrives. Mace in one hand, the other on a holstered gun he announces, "The dog bites me; I'll pepper spray it."

"She isn't going to bite you. I've been here with her for an hour," regret at making the call beginning to creep into my heart.

"The dog makes a move toward me; I'll pepper spray it."

Oh, my god, I think to myself. W*ho is this guy?* "*She,* she's a girl, and she won't bite you. I will put her in your car." I pick her up, taking a quick look inside her mouth first. Puppy teeth. She has all of her puppy teeth. Starving and about five months old. Someone surely is missing this puppy. I put her in the back of the squad car. More regret. "What happens to her now," I ask.

"Euthanized in the morning."

"What did you just say? That can't be true. The shelter is a no-kill shelter. What are you saying? I don't understand."

"I am *just kidding*. She goes to the pound. You can call in the morning." *Just kidding? Who says things like this? What peace officer says things like this?* Thoughts of Luke swirl in my head and heart. More regret filling every cell of my being. I considered opening the door and taking her out of the car, but I feared the figure of authority standing nearby. "Let her out of the car. I will take her home."

"Nope, once in the car they stay in the car. You can call the pound in the morning." He returned to the car without another word and was gone. *What just happened? Why did I let him take her away?* I sit back in the ditch and look at the few pictures I had taken. *Don't worry girlie. I will get you out of there tomorrow.* A week would pass before I would see her again.

A call to the pound in the morning confirmed my guess at her age, just about five months old. Her body condition scored one on the 1 to 9 scale; almost twenty percent below her ideal body weight. And no, I cannot come to visit her, have her back, or bring her food. "She's fine," I am told. Starved, covered with ticks, scars, and scabs with a collar imbedded in her neck I consider the word 'fine.' The woman on the phone must have read my thoughts. "I cut the collar off and put some Frontline on her. She's fine." Knowing the conversation will go nowhere toward the puppy's greater good for the second time in twelve hours I ask, "What happens to her now?"

"Here for seven days, then to the Humane Society if no one claims her. Someone picked up her brother near where you found this one. The puppies were dumped. No one is looking for her.

She'll be at the Humane Society next week."

"If no one is looking for her, why can't I take her home now?" My chest tightens at the answer. "Procedure. If I break the rules for you, I have to break them for everyone." A cartoon-like image of me chasing my tail comes to mind, and I give up the fight. At least with this person. Deanna is next. Founder and president of the local shelter and the dear friend of a friend, I know Deanna will get girl-puppy, already named Ellie, out of there for me. Perhaps. Pleading Ellie's case, including the rude behavior of the city cop, she shuts me down with the same logic.

"You'll have to wait for her Cindi. I know you, and I know you are a champion for dogs. I know that whatever horrors she probably faced, you will help her heal. I know you and Chris will give her a good home. If I break the rules for you, I'll set a precedent that I don't want to deal with. There are reasons for our protocol. Good reasons. Jacque found the brother. She kept him, and he's a handful for her. No one is looking for these puppies. They were dumped. Your Ellie will be here for you next week. Be patient.

Please tell me again about the responding officer's behavior. That is something I do wish to deal with." We had talked for a bit longer before I returned home to my three Labradors to let them know that the pound puppy called Ellie would be coming home soon.

Be patient. Deanna is not the only person in my life who is aware of my lack of patience. Once again thinking and not feeling, I proclaimed that I would foster Ellie until she was ready to be adopted by a new family. A close friend chastised me, "Of course Luke sent her to see if you've learned the universal lesson of shifting the paradigm of how animals are perceived and treated by humans. And she is black and Lab'ish looking, your favorite dog type. That is no accident. Why wouldn't you keep her? Fostering is *not* who you are. Remember Kato? How would this be any different? You know you will fall in love with her. Why does she have to stay at the pound? Adopt her now. Live the new paradigm of believing that a higher power sends you those who are supposed to be with you. You are not meant to do animals part time. That only reinforces that they are not feeling, emotional beings who become attached and feel safe; especially a rescue dog who will learn to trust you. How do you then send a dog like that to a new owner even if that owner is a nice person? What does that say to the dog? So, let me be the first to congratulate you on your new puppy. What is her name?"

Yes, I was already in love with Ellie, and she was not even home with us yet. My friend was right; I cannot do animals part time. I practiced patience for one week and was at the door of the Humane Society the moment Ellie arrived. More rules to practice patience by; Ellie could not go home with me until after she was spayed. My arguments were again bouncing off of the brick wall of protocol. My promises to take her to my vet and have her spayed, ignored, along with my anger that Ellie had to spend another week sleeping alone in a kennel in the quarantine building as a presumed unvaccinated rabies risk. "You can visit her every day, and you can take her home the day of her surgery." The pretzel logic that I could play with her every day, out of her quarantine kennel and surely about to bite me and infect me with rabies, again brought spinning visions of tail chasing and deep wonder at the world in which I live.

I visited Ellie every day for seven days. I taught her about toys. Ellie didn't know about toys. That first day at the shelter, I showed her a big basket full of toys. She showed no interest. "Toys, Ellie, to play with." I tossed a tennis ball. Nothing. Squeaked a squeaky toy. Nothing. Threw a fluffy, stuffed animal toy across the floor. Nothing. She only stood next to the basket staring at me. Pouring the entire basket out on the floor, I ran around tossing toys and singing to her. She clumsily bounded around after me, then jumped up and grabbed my sleeve. "No, Ellie. No teeth." Bringing my energy level down, I considered how quickly she had elevated. *Oh, Luke, who have you sent me?* I wondered, possibly out loud.

Ellie and I walked around inside the big building learning about the leash. Ellie was terrified of the leash. Letting it drag across the floor, she relaxed but only a little; when it was in my hand, she panicked. We worked slowly, the leash hanging freely from Ellie's collar, and I discarded the heavy leather lead choosing

15

instead a thin, nylon wisp of a leash that floated along beside her.

Ellie's first day at the shelter I gave her a bath, lathering her up from head to toe, scrubbing the ticks and scabs and grime from her mostly black coat. Afraid at first and struggling to avoid the water, I sang to her and she settled. As she had done that first evening, the night Ellie found me, she solemnly considered me. Her amber eyes were searching, looking deeply into my soul; perhaps to see, to truly see, if I was safe. It was becoming evident that Ellie did not see humans as safe, and she seemed to have a real fear of water.

Bath finished, her ears cleaned, and her nails trimmed, a now clean, but still really skinny pup looked at me as if asking, *Now What?* Food! Every day that week I brought Ellie extra meals and treats; cans and cans of quality food and giving her extra kibble from the large bin of a mix of all sorts of puppy food donated by well-meaning people. Ellie and I romped and played and sometimes just sat together on the concrete floor of the big building. Ellie gazed at me with eyes filled with gratitude. When I was nearby, she did everything she could to be at my side, never letting me out of sight.

The day before Ellie's scheduled surgery, I gave her another bath. She was only slightly more accepting of her second bath, fear of the water again filling her eyes. Her body was rigid, her jaw set. Ellie trusted me but would have bolted if released. Gently but quickly I bathed her knowing that another bath wouldn't be possible until after her sutures had dissolved. The lesions and infected bites and scabs that covered her body were healing, the blackest black of her coat beginning to shine. Softly humming as I rinsed her, the water carried away dirt that felt heavy with fear and pain. Wrapping Ellie in a big towel, I sat on the floor with her and covered us both with a thick, quilted blanket.

It's only water, Ellie. What happened?

Laughing. They are laughing and laughing, but I can't breathe. I am under the water, and the water is moving. Scared. I am scared. I am scared, and I can't breathe, and I think I might die. I wanted to die. Then they let me breathe again. I didn't die. Laughing. They are laughing, and I am in the air again. Then the water comes back. My body was fighting... I mean, what body doesn't fight to stay alive? My body was fighting, and then I thought, 'It's over, OK I'm dead now.' And then they would stop choking me, and I would be alive again. They would do different things to me where I would be just about dead. But I didn't die. I wanted to die, but I didn't die.

So I... I try to function within that. I am trying to function.

Ellie was showing me pictures of being thrown into a river with a rope tied around her neck. The tiny puppy couldn't swim, and she wasn't strong enough to keep her head above the moving water. Over and over and over again she was pulled out by the rope, hung by the neck, and thrown back into the river.

Oh, Ellie. How much more did you endure? It is no wonder that you are afraid of the water and the leash. I was laughed at too, Ellie. But no one ever threw me in a river. They mocked me, Ellie. They shunned me, and I built a brick wall around my heart to shut them out. I chose to close my heart. You are still a puppy, Ellie, and I promise you I will help you heal your heart; and you can help me heal, soften and open my own.

In one afternoon with Ellie I had been given a glimpse of the abuse she suffered; apparently at the hands of young boys. Perhaps by the boy that she had heard being abused.

My heart hurts...I lived with these people, and one of them was a boy. I don't know that I ever want to see that boy again. And then I think sometimes, sometimes I would hear that boy being abused. Everyone in the house was abused...was...crazy.

A sad pattern of neglect and abuse. What other pain would this puppy show me? Although her time alone in the woods had left the young puppy starving and bug-bitten, I was beginning to believe that the day Ellie was abandoned to fend for herself alone in a dark forest, barely four months old, was the day that saved her life. Sooner or later those games of torture that Ellie had endured would have gone too far, and a dead puppy would have been pulled out of the river.

Ellie was spayed by one of the local veterinarians, and I was there to retrieve her the moment she woke from anesthesia. Settling her into several clean, soft blankets next to me in my truck, and presenting her with a pretty pink collar so that she would not be mistaken for a boy dog, I sat with her for the longest time not going anywhere. Ellie and me sitting together quietly as she snoozed off the groggy effects of surgery. Clock time disappeared as we sat immersed in silence, and our hearts felt the truth of knowing that our journey together was just beginning. Again. Our spirits recognizing one another from both in this time and time past. *Luke?? Is that you?* My questioning thought was filled with wonder. I could feel Luke's spirit *in Ellie*. How could this be? Ellie was already alive when Luke passed over. Some time later I would learn about 'walk-ins.' Luke's spirit most certainly did 'walk-in' to Ellie the day I met her there in a ditch next to the culvert she called home. Stroking Ellie's velvet black fur, bringing my mind back from the silent space we had shared, I started my truck and drove Ellie home.

THE HORSE BLESSING

The next morning dawned clear and cold; frost covered trees and grass reflecting bright sunshine. Plans had been made for Ellie to meet a friend and her dogs. The same friend who had scolded me for thinking I would foster Ellie. Arriving at the ranch, Ellie and I found no humans or dogs; there was no note letting me know of a change in plans. A beautiful gray mare who I had known for a few years was lying in the yard near the house. She was preparing to leave her body. Four days from this day, she would pass. A twenty-five-year-old quarter horse gelding, her soul mate, stood over her.

I sat down in the grass just a few feet away; Ellie curled up in my lap. Sending my heart to the horses, the four of us shared the warmth of the sunshine and the pain of goodbye. Ellie was calm in the presence of the big animals. I knew these horses and felt safe sitting on the ground, vulnerable, with a dog in my lap. The gelding regarded us for a long moment, then stepped away from his friend. He walked directly toward us and stopped with his front hooves under my crossed legs, the long bones of his forelegs touching my knees.

This magnificent horse had been the first to show me that horses can be both teachers and healers for humans, and I trusted him. His strong, solid body standing over us, he lowered his head to Ellie. Her eyes locked with mine, she showed no fear. "It's okay Ellie, this is August." August breathed deeply into Ellie's belly, touching her with his soft muzzle for a long, long minute. I know this is a sacred moment; a horse-blessing for Ellie from a horse who was heartbroken by the illness of his partner.

Looking into his thoughtful eyes, I thanked him. He stood over us for several minutes before returning to his vigil. Sitting surrounded by their peace and their love, Ellie napped in my lap. Ellie, blessed by a horse.

An hour later we slipped away. Ellie not meeting my friend and her dogs; not this day or any other. Like the little girl who so many times in her life turned around to find herself alone, to find that something or someone deeply loved had gone away, one day I turned around and my friend and her horses were gone.

DOCTORS & DNA

How did we get all of this space??? I like that. We run around. No one is running away. We are just running and running and running. And it is FUN running around with other dogs! Not running away, just running around.

Winter brings with it a frozen, snow-covered lake. Eighty-two acres of lake ice surrounded by pine forests and tamarack bog. This is the space that Ellie loves to have around her. Perplexed by her question as I was sitting in my loft office with Labrador Olive at my feet and Ellie in the living room below, my gaze intuitively went to the windows, toward our frozen lake.

It's the lake, Ellie. Is this what you are asking?

Yes, yes. Outside there is a lot of space.

Yes, Ellie, we live next to a lake. Water in the summer and frozen, extra space for you in the winter. Like a vast field for you to play in. With that Ellie let out a great big sigh.

Ahhhhhhhhhhh, thank you.

I smile at the realization that Ellie believes we somehow made all of the extra space just for her. *You're welcome, big girl. You are very welcome.*

Ellie couldn't distinguish between the summer 'lake' and winter 'frozen playland just for her.' Thrown repeatedly into a river as a young puppy, she was terrified of open water.

Ellie *never* ventured down to the lakeshore and into the water with the Labradors spring, summer or fall. Never.

Frozen lake during winter, however, meant fun! Each morning, my happy pack and I would meet our neighbors from the other side of the lake along with their three dogs. Altogether, seven dogs; five Labs plus Ellie and Scout, the adopted ones. On one particularly perfect morning, winter sun dancing on powdery new snow, the dogs ran together with abandon; ears and tails were flowing as they loped across the lake.

Suddenly, Ellie collapsed. One moment she was running fast and free, then, in an instant, flat out lateral on the snow. Frantically I yelled, "Ellie!" skiing quickly toward her. "Ellie! Ellie! Ellie!" **"E L L I E COME BACK!!!!!"** She bolted upright, then sank back to her haunches reaching a paw out to where I sat next to her in the snow. "What's happening, Ellie?" I am distraught. Thankfully very close to our house, I said goodbye to the neighbors and hurried my dogs in off of the lake.

Ellie is weak, her gums pale. As I rush her to the veterinarian, she lies listless in the back of my truck, her breathing shallow and raspy. Blood work, radiographs and physical exam inconclusive; the vet referred us to a cardiologist in Minneapolis.

Committed to giving Ellie the same level of care as the Labradors, we scheduled an ultrasound and echocardiogram. Advised to keep Ellie quiet, with no running and running and running, I kept Ellie on a leash for her daily exercise. She would watch me with sad, accusing eyes when I left her indoors while the other dogs ran free on the lake. Dejected, she would sulk away curling up on her bed as we walked out the door.

A few weeks later we drove Ellie several hours to meet the specialist. Ellie was very polite and cautious while in the big medical facility. The building was huge with every diagnostic tool available. Immaculate surgery suites, exam rooms, comfortable waiting areas, private grieving areas and a staff of doctors, technicians and administrators capable of dealing with trauma, diagnoses, and all things related to the physical bodies of dogs and cats.

Ellie was lifted up onto a small exam table, and an assistant shaved her chest and abdomen for the procedures. It was an unusual table, quite narrow for such a large dog. Ellie needed to lie on her side in a very specific position for all of the machines to work properly. It took a bit of time to get her adjusted just so. Talking softly to her, letting her know everything was okay, she yielded to the doctor examining her, and to the wires and electrodes that were attached to her body. Ellie's ears perked up, and her head cocked with intense curiosity when she heard the sound of her heartbeat. The volume on the ultrasound machine was set quite high, and the sound of Ellie's heartbeat filled the small room. I smiled at this, and my own heart warmed, filled with love for this resilient puppy.

The tests showed no apparent abnormalities. Ellie's sudden collapse was determined to be either a single episode of a cardiac nature that left no scar tissue or other permanent damage or a collapse caused by electrolyte imbalance due to severe malnutrition over the first several months of her life. Ellie's malnutrition had been obvious from the moment I met her, but it had not occurred to me that this could still be causing her harm. She appeared so big, strong, and healthy on the outside. Ellie's diet was evaluated and adjusted, adding whole foods and supplements, and feeding four times per day to decrease the risk of hypoglycemia. Ellie loved this!

Not long after her visit to the heart specialist, Ellie had surgery to remove several of her adult teeth. Coming in seemingly fine after losing her puppy teeth, soon four molars and one premolar were rotting and dying. There had been a small stick wedged along the roof of Ellie's mouth when I found her. The stick, other than being an uncomfortable nuisance, didn't seem to bother her. Discovered the day I gave Ellie her first bath, it was removed and tossed in the trash. No one gave it a second thought until Ellie's adult teeth came in and quickly died. Minus five big teeth, Ellie had now undergone two significant medical procedures predicated by the neglect and abuse of her first twenty weeks of life. Whether purposely shoved into her mouth, or finding its way to where it was lodged by her chewing on it while alone and wandering, it was a gooey, black, smelly, rotten piece of pulp when I pulled it out of her mouth. That stick had been there for quite some time.

Ellie continued to run, romp, play and grow. Curiosity about her ancestry grew along with her body, and we ordered a DNA test kit. Living with Labradors for many years, I knew that Ellie was not a Lab mix as many 'mostly black with a little white' shelter dogs are labeled. After many spirited discussions with others, each who insisted, without a doubt, that our Ellie was a Mastiff mix - a Dane mix - a Pitbull mix, we submitted Ellie's saliva sample. So, who is this big girl we call Ellie? Mostly St. Bernard, a little less but still a lot Great Dane, a little bit of Boxer, and a tiny bit of Dachshund. Dachshund? Could there possibly be any Dachshund in this gigantic dog? There were many amusing conversations around Ellie's great-great-great-probably-grandfather DNA. A common response to Ellie's Dachshund genetics, "The only way there is any Dachshund in her is if she swallowed one!" Ellie the 120-pound wiener dog.

The St. Bernard in her family tree was becoming more and more apparent as her head and facial features matured. Her skull is massive. The Great Dane's tendency toward sitting in their human's favorite chair was also dominant. Ellie took over my big, comfortable reading chair offering to share it with me only if she could sit in my lap. As I can barely breathe when she sits in my lap, which looks more like Ellie sitting *on* my lap, legs and most of the rest of me, I gave her my chair.

TROUBLE

Ellie's first winter went on, and the snow-loving St. Bernard-mix joyfully created chase games with the other dogs. Roaring up the great big snow plow piles, she would spin around at the top and dare any other to claim her mountain peak. Scout, who was much faster than all of the Labs and Ellie, raced through the snow-covered bogs, Tamarack stands and the wide-open space of the frozen lake. Ellie gave chase, squeaking and squealing and howling in frustration at her inability to catch the speedy dog. Ellie was fast, just not fast enough! And Ellie didn't like to lose any game. She would give chase for a little while, and then charge off to engage one of the other dogs in a game of snow wrestle. No one could win snow wrestle with

Ellie. She would sit her big body on top of her worthy opponent until they wiggled their way free. She was now about nine months old.

One morning after an hour of running and playing with her dog friends, Ellie's Labrador siblings, Olive and Kato, were engaged in their own game of tug-o-war with a big stick. Never to be left out of a game, Ellie bounded toward the two. Referred to as The Queen of the Pack, Olive is a good leader, always aware and vigilant. The small, fifty-pound Lab released the stick and squared off at Ellie showing her teeth and nothing more. Olive was clearly telling Ellie that this was Kato and Olive's game. Ellie was not invited to play. Ellie pounced, and the snow became a blur of black fur, teeth, and snarling. There in an instant, I pulled Ellie away. Olive was visibly unnerved, and she was angry. The perhaps foolish little queen threatened Ellie again. Ellie lurched toward her, but I somehow held her back. *Wow, Ellie*, I thought.

The speed and ferocity with which she attacked were completely inappropriate for the message Olive had sent. Showing teeth is a dog's nonverbal message asking for space, setting a boundary. Properly socialized puppies and dogs learn this at a young age from their parents and littermates. Ellie seemed not to understand this. A proper response would have been to respect the boundary and turn away. Especially since Ellie's pack leader had delivered the message. An aggressive attack, grabbing Olive securely by the neck and intending to do great harm, was anything but proper.

Clipping a leash on Ellie's collar, I led her and the rest of my gang home. It appeared I had a problem to solve and my mind was racing. Did Ellie have *any* canine social skills? Until now no other dog had challenged her or had any reason to challenge her. Because of her size, most other dogs gladly allowed her the role of playground leader. Many months had passed without incident. The thought of having an aggressive dog in our multi-dog household was troubling, especially a dog as big as Ellie. All dogs are powerful. Ellie was miniature horse-horsepower powerful. Now healthy, strong, and heavily muscled, if Ellie chose to aggress on anyone or anything, the result would be bad. Or worse.

For most of the past 25 years, there have been two, three or four dogs in our home. The occasional dog fight was not unknown to us. All of our dogs until Ellie, however, understood dog-to-dog language and knew exactly where they stood in the pack hierarchy. Most disagreements were displays of teeth, hackles, and aggressive barking in one another's face usually started by one of two things: space (or the lack thereof) or the ownership of a favored toy. The loser of these skirmishes would wisely back down and slink off to a quiet place to repair a bruised doggie ego, and I would follow looking closely at face, ears, and neck for any wounds. Rarely did I find an injury needing more than a friendly pat on the head, assuring that all was going to be okay. Before long the fight was forgotten, and they would be off to romp and play, swim, or rest together on a favorite dog bed.

Ellie's behavior around the Lab's game of stick tug was excessive in its aggression. She ignored many levels of canine communication in her response to the boundary set by Olive. If Ellie had chosen to challenge Olive rather than turning away and yielding to the message, a more appropriate response would have been a return of the toothy sneer and maybe a growl. Responding as she had, grabbing Olive by the neck and proceeding to pummel the petite Labrador into the snow, a Labrador who then gave signals of *I surrender, don't kill me!* was deeply troubling. I now had an aggressive member in my canine family. A puppy who was not yet one year old; whose past I had only glimpses of; who did not spend her puppyhood in my loving care; who had spent weeks and weeks alone as a not yet twenty-week-old puppy on her own in the forest. A puppy who had called a culvert home, a hiding place in the dark where who knew what may have stalked and frightened her. She didn't live in that wild world any longer, but the effects of that traumatic time were still with her.

Ellie's scars were more than physical. Ellie needed emotional healing too. The emotional ups and downs of the next weeks and months would bring both pain and healing; for Ellie, for Chris and me, for the other dogs. Hearts would break wide open, and healing would begin.

TRIGGERED

Most of the time I am saying 'Move Away! Back Away! Move Away! Back Away! Move Away!!! Move A-WAY!!!'...Over and over and louder and louder, FOUR HUNDRED TIMES Move A-way! I become obsessive. I feel that I am giving all of the other dogs notice, Ok? I don't know that they should be surprised at *anything*. They should just listen to me and MOVE AWAY!

February 1, 2014. Olive's seventh birthday; Ellie's second winter. *Huh,* I thought as I allowed all four dogs to bound through the door together after a fun romp in the snow. *Ellie seems a little UP about something.* What happened next was chaos. Ellie bolted across the room and latched firmly onto Olive's neck, shaking her while Olive screamed and fought to get away. Our oldest dog, Jack, got out of the way, hiding in a corner. Kato was barking and spinning and hopping around Ellie, begging her to stay present, to not hurt Olive, to stop putting her teeth in Olive. Ellie had been triggered and gone away. She did not hear him. Chris flew down the stairway and separated them, hauling Ellie off of her victim and dragging her into another room. Olive disappeared.

Furious and eliciting a torrent of expletives, trembling as adrenaline raced through my body, I yelled and screamed, trying to shake off my trauma; trauma that would surely find its way deep into my body. *"I DON'T NEED THIS ELLIE! WHY WHY WHY WHY WHY?!? WHAT HAPPENED TO YOU, ELLIE????"* The love in my heart for this dog felt like daggers slicing me to pieces as I burst into tears at the realization that this couldn't continue. I turned my back on Ellie and left her to find Olive.

On the third floor of the house, as far away as physically possible from the scene of the brutal attack, Olive hid under a bed. Her body curled tightly and pressed into a corner; I crawled under. Olive's eyes are filled with terror and accusation, my heart breaking yet again. "Yes, I know. I failed you again, Olive. Please come out. I need to see what she did to you." Glaring at me, she didn't budge. Pulling her gently out from underneath the bed, I examine her neck. Several deep punctures and two deep tears from being shaken. It is late morning. Saturday. Olive needs emergency attention.

I call the vet, praying that he will be in this late on a mid-winter Saturday. A technician answered the phone; it was one minute before the clinic's closing time. Trying to verbalize what had just happened through my tears and anger, I am interrupted. "Bring her in. Now!" Scooping up Olive and leaving all else behind, I rushed my petite, torn-up Labrador to the animal hospital.

I, yes, yes; definitely fighting energy in me. And I just don't know if I will not be triggered again. And I know that that is the big question here. The question is, can I... Can I have a life with other beings? Can I have a life with other beings that don't always follow MY rules?

Ellie's fight, flight, or freeze response when triggered was very charged, set high on fight. She rushed toward anything and everything that startled her. The few times she completely disassociated were always accompanied by blinding fury and rage directed toward Olive.

On a daily basis, seemingly the tiniest thing startled her into lightning fast action; birds, squirrels, grasshoppers, Chris or me coming in from outdoors. Fully present, Ellie rushed Chris and me from wherever she might be in the house, thankfully with eyes shining and tail wagging as her love and gratitude for us have never wavered. The birds, squirrels, and grasshoppers, however, were often victims of her speed, agility, and jaws. Surely her sparse meals when alone in the forest consisted of an insect or two, maybe a squirrel; most certainly a bird or many based on the speed and efficiency with which she chased, and sometimes caught, songbirds. Ellie learned, "No Chase, Ellie," and soon was content to watch the birds and other small critters that gathered at the feeders as she lay in the sun on the deck. Her struggles with Olive would continue a while longer.

I can't stand that Olive won't LISTEN TO ME!!! I hate her. I hate her when she doesn't listen to me! NO ONE listens to me. They didn't listen to me. They didn't listen to me when I told them it hurt. They didn't listen. No one listened to me. They didn't give a damn about me. They didn't listen to me at all.

No, Ellie, they didn't give a damn about you. They didn't care about you at all. I'm sorry for that, Ellie; for the hurt that other people caused you. They didn't listen to you when you told them it hurt. Honestly, Ellie, they didn't care that it hurt. They were hurting you on purpose. They strangled you. They threw you into that raging river. They stomped on your tender, young puppy paws. They poked you all over your body with something very sharp. They kicked you. In the head. In the chest. In the stomach. They hung you up until you were unconscious, then waited for you to wake up so they could do it again. And again. And again. They didn't listen to you, Ellie. Some people are cruel. Cruel beyond words. I can feel your heart hurting Ellie. I will always listen to you, Ellie. I will hold you and fill all of the empty spaces with love. I will help you remove those blocks, Ellie; at your pace and in your time. You are loveable, Ellie. So special and I can feel the love in you. You can love now, and I think you are beginning to know that. And what about Olive, Ellie? Can you love Olive, too? Can you love Olive as much as you love me?

Well, sometimes I do get along with her. And I'm like, 'OK, Allllll right, you're the leader, and I'm going to go along with this.' And then I'm good, and I am well behaved. And I don't think you feel any tension from me. But then I'll just have moments. I'm not even exactly sure how they start. I feel like I'm back trying to be alive again and I just flip backward in time...And it's just some little trigger. Sometimes it's different. I don't even know what; it's not something exact. Like I don't think you can even say, 'Oh, it's THIS' or that you can say to each other, 'Hey if we do this, or don't do that, Ellie's going to be fine.' I don't think you can pinpoint that. I can't. Can you? Am I right or wrong about that?

Ellie chose to heal. That her spirit body had communicated to me this contemplation of her triggers left no doubt in my mind that Ellie was suffering from Canine Post-Traumatic Stress Disorder, C-PTSD. Admitting that she could not pinpoint what triggered her; that it was not always the same thing or only one thing that began her process of flipping back in time and fighting, and then directing the question back to me was proof enough for me that she wanted to heal. It was no accident that this rejected puppy turned big beautiful dog found her way to me. My fascination with energy and the body's energy channels allowed me to see Ellie; to see the entirety of her being instead of the fearful, aggressive giant that many others saw looking only with their eyes. Ellie's energy body was not healthy. There was tension in her head, her paws, her belly. She held tension from abuse throughout her body, but especially in her head. The side of her face, her forehead, her sinuses, all were energetically pinched and blocked. Ellie continued to hold much tension and pain in her head, even after the surgery to remove her diseased teeth. Her chest and belly felt hollow and empty. Ellie had repeatedly been kicked in the chest, and her toes pinched and stomped on. Ellie was filled with fear and anger, the hollow spaces of her energy body held only dark, low emotions: fear, anger, hatred, and sadness that was nearly paralyzing to me. Of all the emotion trapped in Ellie's body, her sadness was most profound.

Why was I unlovable to them?

Ellie asked this question on many occasions, always with deep, sobbing pain rising within her and within those of us who could hear her. Ellie one hundred percent wanted to be here with me and Chris and the other dogs; wanted us all to love her; wanted to be lovable. Her heart hurt. She felt empty, yet she wanted to be filled with love. Every cell of her being needed to be filled with love.

HEALING

Why was I unlovable to them?

So many empty spaces. Your heart feels empty, Ellie; empty of love and filled with deep sadness. Not so long ago, my own heart was empty; empty of love and filled with deep sadness. Ancient sorrow. Sadness that was foreign to me; it was not entirely my own. The torture and abuse you endured as a young puppy, suffered every single day for so many weeks before literally being thrown away, have left you hollow. Hollow where they kicked you; hollow where they poked holes in you; hollow where they squeezed your face and head; hollow where they choked the young voice out of you. They don't know love, Ellie. They were unable to love you.

The energies of Ellie's body were unbalanced; full of fighting energy, distrust, and rage. Ellie's rage had triggers, PTSD-like triggers. Triggers that I could feel in my body. When Ellie was triggered, she disassociated and then attacked. Later she would come back, tail wagging, not knowing what had happened; not knowing the damage she had done. This behavior left the other dogs and humans in the house stressed and in a state of hypervigilance; especially Olive who bore the brunt of Ellie's rage.

Ellie's anxieties were many: fear of water - lakes, streams, rivers, puddles, rain; fear of the dark; fear of the forest; fear of men; fear of young boys - an actual *terror* of young boys; fear of enclosed spaces. A twenty-four by twenty-four-foot room was, to Ellie, enclosed space. Ellie bristled and then rushed at virtually anything that surprised her, from an insect to someone entering her home. Her response to all stimuli was to push her energy, physical and emotional, *toward* what she feared. Ellie had grown into a giant dog. Her adult weight nearing 120 pounds, she was powerful, and she was fast.

Knowing how Ellie was hurting on so many levels and how she responded when triggered, choosing the right path for her healing process seemed incredibly important. Adequate space was imperative to Ellie. Her worst episodes of disassociating occurred indoors when triggered by claustrophobia. Because of her trauma as a puppy nearly drowning in a river and being repeatedly choked by a rope around her neck, Ellie only truly relaxed when she was outdoors, by herself, with plenty of air and space around her.

What do you need from me, Ellie? Where do we even begin to help you through all of this trapped anger and rage? I want to help you Ellie, but you need to help me understand. What does Ellie want?

I need a consistent environment. I need a SAFE and CONSISTENT environment, and I don't want anyone to argue with me over what I feel I need. When someone argues with me, I feel like I am going to die and I just start fighting. And I don't always know exactly what I am fighting. And then it's like...then I come to, and I have to see what happened.

Ellie's environment at home with us was certainly consistent and safe. Her early days before she was left on her own were anything but safe, and more likely resembled utter chaos than consistency. Those early days were tormenting Ellie, and it seemed she was trapped in her puppy-past. On more than one occasion Ellie had shown her dislike of not being in charge. She didn't want anyone to argue with her; she told the other dogs, Four-hundred times move away! She hated that Olive didn't listen to her, she hated that no one listened to her, that they didn't care about her at all.

The continual struggle between Olive and Ellie needed to be resolved. The two dogs tolerated one another when they were outside together. Indoors, Olive stayed out of Ellie's way, most of the time hiding in the loft office.

Much time had been devoted to Ellie; training Ellie, acupressure and other healing for Ellie, cardiologists for Ellie, surgery for Ellie, socialization for Ellie. Realizing that Olive, too, was suffering, I asked her what she wanted. I was not prepared for what followed.

WHY ARE YOU LISTENING TO ELLIE?!?!?!?! STOP IT! DON'T LISTEN TO HER! I'VE BEEN HERE THE LONGEST AND I AM THE LEAD DOG HERE DAMNIT!!!

YOU BE QUIET OLIVE!!! Ellie immediately replied; she was getting angry.

In an instant I understood. They had been energetically bickering continuously for more than a year; arguing over leadership, arguing over who controlled the space that Ellie and Olive shared. If Ellie and Olive were speaking to one another with our human language it might sound something like this:

Ellie - Na Na Na you said that.

Olive - NO, I said that.

Ellie - Ok back up back up back up.

Olive - No, YOU back up.

Ellie - No, you can't say that.

Olive – Yes, I can.

Ellie – No, you can't.

Olive - But this is MY space.

Ellie – No, it's not. You back up back up

BACK UP!!!

At the time, eleven-year-old Jack and three-year-old Kato had always listened when Ellie began to feel triggered and tell the other dogs, MOVE AWAY MOVE AWAY Move Away Move Away move away move away...
FOUR HUNDRED TIMES MOVE AWAY!

Jack's only comment concerning Ellie? I don't want any trouble. No trouble!

And Kato, I'm a baby, I'm a baby, I'm a baby! I'm getting out of the way!

So, both boy dogs more or less telling the girls, Whoever wants to boss us around is just fine! Olive was furious with them, and me, for listening to Ellie. Olive is a good leader and a good top dog. She has more patience than any dog I have ever known and she understands that physically Ellie outweighs her by one hundred and twenty percent. Ellie has a powerhouse advantage, and Olive knows it. She continued,

I've avoided a lot of fights because of these different things and I just feel that it would give everyone peace of mind if Ellie lived someplace else. I know that this is very, very hard for you to hear because you don't want to abandon Ellie; she's already been abandoned. You found her. You fed her. She is healthy. She is SO strong and fit. You are her saving angel, and she does adore you, but if anyone is going anywhere, it's Ellie. It's not any of us. Because we were here first. This is one hundred percent our home, and it's not one hundred percent Ellie's home. And, she's the one having problems with the other dogs. It would be better for her to be someplace else where she is the *only* dog, she can have *all* the space, and the humans would listen to her. There would be nothing else to challenge her place, and she would never feel worried that she wouldn't have control over it. That is what I think. We are all walking on eggshells here wondering 'When is Ellie going to go off?' That is the question. And I don't believe that the question is whether she is ever going to go off again. She is. She is going to go off again. Is she going to go off a lot? No. And, she can be very sweet and very amazing and very funny; ok, she has a lot of good things. But it's 'when?' Because it will happen. Something is going to trigger her, or I'm going to say something, and I'm not going to allow her to push me around. I'm just, NO, I won't. And, I have been incredibly patient with Ellie. I have tried to work this out, I have. I just don't want to get killed over this dog! And I'm not going to be the bottom of the pecking order. It's not going to be the Ellie show. It's not. I know that's what she wants. It's not going to be the Ellie show...

Ellie interrupted, her words filled with fear,

Don't you know...DON'T YOU KNOW that IF YOU DON'T LISTEN TO ME... If I don't HAVE MY SPACE... Don't you know that if you don't listen to me and I don't have my space I'm going to end up outside again, alone, with hundreds of punctures all over me and I'm going to be starving to death?!?!?!? Don't you know that IF YOU DON'T LISTEN TO ME, I COULD DIE?!?!?!?!?

Okay, okay. Ellie. Olive. Settle down. Ellie, you are not going to end up outside again, alone, with hundreds of punctures all over you and starving to death. Olive, thank you for speaking up; you've had an awful lot on your mind. Both of you come with me. We are going for a walk together, and we are going to work this out.
For now, no one is going anywhere. Here's what we are going to do...

Over the next many weeks and months, much time and attention were focused on Ellie and Olive, on repairing the damage that had been done by their continual bickering and by Ellie's rage. The two dogs went on long walks with me; some days on leash, but more often free to roam and run together with me hiking along behind. More or less they got along, but still only when outdoors. Olive did not trust Ellie inside of the house. Outside they were becoming friends. Inside, they lived on separate floors. Olive in the third-floor loft office, Ellie in her chair in front of the fireplace just below. Ellie was not allowed in Olive's room. Olive, free to go wherever she wished, continued to choose the loft. Unless Ellie was separated from Olive by yet one more floor, in her doggie bedroom on the lowest level of our home, Olive stayed upstairs. Her seclusion worried me.

Once again, I felt as though I had failed one dog who had been with me for many years, and another who had come to me psychologically and physically damaged. My mind was consumed with healing these deep wounds, with somehow closing the seemingly insurmountable chasm that separated the two of them. At this point, Ellie seemed to be doing better than Olive, perhaps because Ellie had no memory of her actions when triggered. Olive remembered every terrifying moment. Inside of the house, repeated gigantic St. Bernard-Great Dane doggie play bows, thirty-inch tail wagging like a flag in a parade, had no effect. Olive observed and ignored the invitations to play. Ellie was Olive's 'outside only' friend, at least for the time being.

With the realization that the path toward healing was indeed going to be long, with many bumps and twists and turns, I saw that I needed to let go of the struggle and allow Ellie and Olive to define their relationship as time passed. My job as their leader and caretaker became crystal clear; keep them safe, work with them, and offer them healing. I released my fear of failure, my worry, my hypervigilance; or so I thought. My perception of my inner state was mistaken.

One morning while out walking with Ellie, I became very aware of my internal space; of exactly how I was feeling and how I reacted to the environment and Ellie. *Am I Ellie's trigger? Is it me, myself being triggered, causing Ellie to react?* It was true! It seemed that every noise, every approaching car, every squirrel or bird that crossed our path was causing me anxiety. Ellie responded by rushing toward each of them. The realization that my anxieties around Ellie – that some inner aspect of myself was more or less hanging on for dear life – that my becoming triggered was triggering her – was a bit of a shock, and also a turning point. I understood that to help Ellie, I must help myself first. The layers of anxiety and fear I held so deeply within needed to be healed.

The following morning, I noticed a Pileated Woodpecker near the edge of the bog. Generally a shy bird, she allowed me to stand nearby and observe her; the methodical *whack-whack-whack* of her powerful beak stripping away the layers of an old Birch tree. She appeared joyful in her work.

You know me to be a shy bird. I offer you this time with me to teach you, to show you how to be diligent, how to be deliberate in your work. Take this back to your Ellie and to your personal work. Work diligently and work from a place of JOY, not sorrow; CONFIDENCE, not fear. Live only for each moment, not hindered by the past or worrying about future. This is the next step on your path.

I thanked the woodpecker for this offering from Spirit and went indoors to my dogs. Ellie and I returned outdoors, and as we walked, I shared these insights with her. Together we returned to the woodpecker and watched her peel away the layers of the old tree. I told Ellie how we might embrace her example of existing only for this moment where there is not space for the laments of the past nor fear of the future. Ellie's tail wagged gently as she observed the bird; watching and perhaps listening as I had, allowing the lesson to be fully realized.

Another autumn was turning toward winter, and there was relative peace and harmony among the dogs. Olive occasionally joined the other dogs in the living room in front of the fireplace but quickly disappeared when Ellie got too close. Outdoors the two of them once again ran together with abandon, but Olive immediately submitted when Ellie claimed a toy or stick that was in Olive's possession. Olive now appeared to be the dog easily triggered; triggered into a fear state that caused her to freeze. Olive was not a fighter. As Ellie showed no signs of aggressing on Olive, I quietly assured Olive that all was well; that she could be Ellie's friend. Then, I explained to Ellie that Olive was afraid; afraid that Ellie might hurt her once again. *Look, Ellie. There's your friend Olive. She's a dog. She's not a boy. She's a dog. She's a little bouncy dog, and she's a very nice dog. She's your friend. She wants to be your friend. Please don't hurt her. Please don't hurt her again.* I feel Ellie's heart breaking, her words filled with pain and tears.

Ohhhhhhhh, I like Olive. I do like Olive. I like everyone here. I don't want to go live anywhere else. She's my friend. I don't want to be a bad dog...I got scared.

Yes, Ellie, you got scared. I know that now. We all know that now. I think even Olive knows. You have a big, loving heart, Ellie. I can feel that. Maybe other people can't feel that, and that is why you found me, Ellie. I can feel your love. You are okay now. Safe. No one will ever harm you again, Ellie. Your world with us is a beautiful, safe place. You can be you, Ellie, and express the great joy that is inside of you.

Ellie next to the culvert she called home October 2012

Ellie's first day at the Northwoods Humane Society –
NHS - following her week-long stay at the Pound
October 2012

Investigating a basket of toys at NHS

Ellie did not know about toys

Taking a treat after having her first bath

Ellie in her kennel at NHS

Ellie's first night at home October 2012

Olive and Ellie December 2012

Jack November 2015

Ellie and Jack 2013

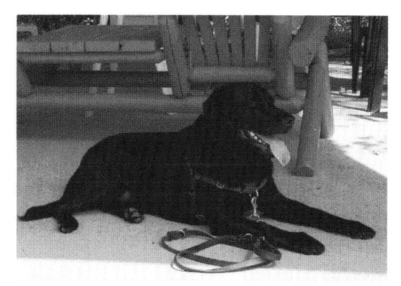

Kato at NHS Spring 2015

Kato 2016

Ellie and Olive Winter 2015 – 2016

Ellie 2015

Clockwise from Ellie: Ellie, Olive, Jack, Kato 2014

Ellie summer 2015

Receiving the message that Ellie needed help
March 2015

Ellie 2016

SISTERS

Olive's eighth birthday; Ellie's third winter. Twelve months had passed since Ellie's PTSD induced attack on Olive. Time heals. Outside on this day, February 1, 2015, Ellie and Olive together bounding through a blanket of new fallen snow. Ellie's long, fluid body; black against the winter white world, moving with grace and incredible speed as she creates a race course through the yard. Running up the snow drifts, then down into the woods toward the creek, across the bog and back up the big hill to where she began, stopping abruptly but not before leaping into the air and flying over Olive. Ellie spins and offers Olive a huge Ellie play bow. Flag tail waving, forelegs longer than my arms planted on the snow, haunches high in the air; Olive returns the bow and they are off! Tearing through Ellie's racetrack creation, stopping to wrestle, Olive jumping on Ellie's massive head, Ellie flopping onto the snow which gives Olive cause to wriggle on her back next to her big little sister. Sisters. Ellie and Olive one year later; they play like this every morning. Running, leaping, play bowing and flying over and under one another until they fall into a pile of black fur, legs, and tails intertwined; resting together on the snow.

During Ellie's third winter, she began to make choices. Good choices. Not always, but most of the time. *What can you do if you feel like you might be triggered, Ellie?*

Well, maybe I could go outside. Or grab a toy. I could grab a toy and own THAT. Or maybe I could just lay down. Lay down and cover my eyes.

Yes, Ellie, you can make choices. You can choose to go outside or look out the window if you can't get to the outside. You can choose to lay down and cover your eyes. You can choose to get

80

a toy and own that. Choices, Ellie. You can choose.

At this time, I was also working one on one with many reactive dogs; shelter dogs with unknown histories as well as my clients' dogs, dogs that lived in loving homes. Reactive to other dogs. Reactive to children. Reactive to strangers. Reactive on leash. Reactive to anyone who came onto their property. It was becoming very clear to me that yes, our dogs can choose. With compassionate training and guidance dogs who, for whatever their circumstance, for whatever or whoever was the cause of their problems, could choose a better way.

Ellie was making many good choices. During their morning romps in the snow, if Olive grabbed a stick, which she now frequently did, and taunted Ellie with it, Ellie chose to drop to the ground, tail high in a play bow. Then, instead of giving chase, she would spin and run around until she found *a different toy*. One of Kato's shredded Frisbees that so fascinated her; or a different stick, one that she could own for herself. Possession of sticks had formerly sent Ellie into the red-zone. Fear would pierce every cell of my being when I felt Ellie's energy elevate to rage over a twig. Now, she was learning to choose, and I encouraged her out loud, *"Good choices, Ellie!"* She understood. Understood that I had been helping her to choose. Assisting her to let go of the past pains and traumas, to drain them away, out of her body, out of her heart, out of her brain so that all of that space could be filled with love.

Later that winter unexpected family commitments, a funeral, and three other trips previously planned caused Chris and me to travel many times within a few months. Ellie began to suffer. Her attachment to me bordered on obsession; she did not like to be physically separated from me by any distance greater than she could see me.

Ellie's internal struggles were beginning to manifest as dis-ease. Our travel schedule had left her with no energy. She became sick each time we returned home; lethargic, terrible diarrhea, her abdomen too painful to touch. She had lost sixteen pounds in four months. My worry was causing her additional stress and increasing her ever-present anxiety. The last trip we were away seven nights. Too long.

Too long for me to be away from my dogs. Too much time for Ellie in a kennel trying so very hard to 'Be a good girl,' until I returned. While meditating on a beach in California, I asked Spirit, '*Ok, it's almost time to go home. What's next?*' The answer startled me. '*ELLIE! ELLIE! ELLIE!*' I asked for clarification, '*The book or the dog?*' '*ELLIE!*'

Seemingly fine while at the boarding kennel, Ellie's stress came roaring out upon my return. The full realization that I must do something more for Ellie consumed my heart. The realization that I had to show her that her world was now a safe place, that she could be ok without me, and that her love for and attachment to me did not need to be intertwined with deep sadness and excessive stress when I had to be away. I also needed to show Ellie that when we *were* home together, she need not be hypervigilant, anxious, and ready to react on my behalf every waking moment.

Ellie's stress was eating her up. She was thin, lethargic, and unhappy. Although we had no further travel plans, Ellie did not know this. She continued to lose weight, and the light had gone from her eyes. A brief moment of playful abandon with Olive each morning was the only time I saw a glimpse of the bright, funny, silly, big goofy girl she used to be. She no longer ran and ran and ran, stopping only to offer that Ellie-sized play bow that could be felt through the earth. A few lackluster bursts of chase and she was done. The remainder of the day she slept. When I held my palm to her belly, she arched away in pain; belly taught, stomach gurgling and churning beneath my hand. She had terrible diarrhea despite medicine and acupressure to ease her pain. *Ellie, Ellie, what is it I am to do to help you?*

As I considered how Ellie was both physically and emotionally nearly three and a half years after our first meeting, and although much progress had been made, I lamented the fact that my gifts of communicating with and healing the animals were of little help to Ellie. I sat with this in meditation for several days. *It's you. YOU are Ellie's problem.* Terrific.

Thinking about our recent trip to California, and how different the energy is there, how much easier it seems to be to exist at a very high vibration when there, I was reminded of a conversation on our last morning by the ocean; the morning I received the message that Ellie needed help. A dear friend, Shanny, wondered out loud a powerful question; simple, yet loaded with possibility. "What's next for you spiritually, Chris and Cin?" Shanny always knows just how to challenge us to move forward on our path. She asks these questions lightly, yet there is an undertone; a subtle sense of urgency that we have much work to do.

As the three of us chatted I, as I had done so many times in the past, lamented at my feelings of hopelessness; that the sea of humanity before my eyes was lost, would never understand, would never have even the first glimmer of waking up. "I never feel like that, Cin! Every person I see, no matter who, I think maybe, just maybe, they have done one teeny tiny beautiful thing." This conversation carried over to my attachment to my personal need to elevate certain friends and family members to where I felt they needed to be. Shanny challenged me, "I wonder how things will shift for you when you lay them down, Cin. You are doing more work than they are. They are on their path. You take care of *yourself*."

The remainder of this particular day was incredible for me. I chose to see the light in everyone, regardless of how dim my perception of their particular light happened to be. My heart lifted, and a sense of perfection replaced my former hopelessness. I chose, energetically, to release my friends and my family to their paths, and to honor them for where and who they are; releasing my need to judge them, fix them, abandon them or heal them. Shanny's response as I shared this with her later, "Wow! You inspire me, Cin. Consider a new way of thinking and being and adopt it. Just like that!"

Considering all of this together, how I had so quickly shifted my energy and my thinking after that conversation with Shanny, I applied this new knowledge to Ellie. Something energetically very powerful was blocking Ellie and blocking my ability to help her heal completely. Again I asked her, *I want to help you Ellie, but you need to help me understand. What does Ellie want?*

WHERE ARE YOU? I feel alone again. I'm waiting and waiting and waiting, and I can't see you. I'm a good girl. You told me to be a good girl, and I AM being a good girl...but these people aren't YOU. I can't see you, and I feel alone. Help me. YOU show me how to heal. I don't know another way. I don't want to be a bad dog.

Ellie was showing me pictures of her sitting in her kennel room while I was away. Dejected and lonely, she believed I had abandoned her; abandoned by the one person who loved her so very much.

So now I looked at Ellie, and I saw myself in her reflection. Holding her head in my hands, I sat with her, my tears spilling onto her muzzle. *Help me, Ellie. Show me how to heal. Maybe it is me who doesn't know another way. Healing Ellie, Healing Me. Let's help one another, Ellie. Let's choose joy, see the light in everyone, and release fear, resentment, and grief. We can let it go, Ellie. Both of us, you and me. Together, two integral pieces of a vast, infinite, interconnected universe. We can let go of our attachment to one another, Ellie. We are all one; always together no matter how far apart we may be on the physical plane. We can let go of our fear of separation, Ellie. And that doesn't mean we love each other any less. Maybe it means we can love each other even more. You don't need me, Ellie. You are already a part of me. We are all the same. You don't need to cause yourself so much trouble, Ellie. Let it go. Let me go. Let it all be, and once again be that funny, silly, exuberant puppy I once knew.*

Ellie fell asleep. Ellie dreamed. She slept for fourteen hours. The next morning, Ellie was brighter. Although it was cold, wet, and windy outside she was almost cheerful on our morning walk. And she passed a normal stool. After days and days of terrible diarrhea, even with medicine, a solid poop was the last thing I expected to see on this walk. Ellie's veterinarian said it might be days before her system would have any motility at all, let alone be back to normal.

Things were shifting for Ellie. I knew that I, myself, had much work to do. As easily and effortlessly as some energetic shifts seem to happen, there were deeper layers of pain within me that would not be easy nor effortless to peel away and shed. Even after years of doing this personal work, and reaching a very high place energetically, there is always more coming to the surface. Clearing away a layer of fear and doubt often reveals a painful memory or buried emotion that had been cleverly hidden by an ever-and-over-protective psyche.

The emotions now revealed were attachment and abandonment. The realization came that these feelings, the energetics of attachment and abandonment, were deeply ingrained within me. Fear of being abandoned causing me to become overly attached; dependent upon things, ideas, habits, people, and dogs. Conditioned by my past, by the residue of the conditioning of my ancestors, I had allowed myself to live in a constant state of deep fear. Fear of loss, fear of being abandoned, fear of not being good enough, smart enough, perfect enough.

The constant state of fear buried deep within me for decades, perhaps even for lifetimes, had left me in a state of hypervigilance. Just like Ellie. Ellie had survived a puppyhood that was defined by fear; continually tortured, living in a constant state of threat. Ellie had been trying to function in an environment of perpetual, relentless, ongoing persecution. That she and I reflected one another so precisely, that our trapped emotion, that which blocked us from moving forward and thriving paralleled one another, was astounding to me. *YOU are Ellie's problem.* Although not the cause of Ellie's initial trauma and pain, I was hindering her forward progress by my failures. My inability to see that I was trapped by an ego that refused to let go, refused to allow healing; unwilling to let go of memories and emotions that no longer served my highest good.

Ellie and I seemed to be stuck in the same place. The message received from Spirit suddenly had deep meaning for both Ellie and me. The message to let go, to let it all go, to let one another go, not in the sense that Ellie must go live somewhere else, but to let our *attachment* to one another go to move forward side by side, with joy.

LAMA KARMA

Help me. YOU show me how to heal. I don't know another way. I don't want to be a bad dog.

The entire weekend had gone wrong. Sunday, November 15, 2015, and now it is me asking a powerful question, "WHY is this dog in my life?" My heart was spilling pain, frustration, and fear. Ellie has just charged our friend. The morning was yet early, and I presumed all were still asleep when I took Olive and Ellie out in the yard to play. The two dogs were playing their favorite game of Chase me Ellie! No - you chase ME Olive. No, wait - I'll chase you after all...racing one another around through the woods in dizzying circles.

"Hey, Cindi!" Everything in my awareness froze, then resumed in slow motion. *Anna. Why is Anna walking up the driveway? Everyone is still sleeping.* Ellie charged, launching all 120 pounds into the air directly at our friend. Moving fast, yet feeling nothing, I got to Ellie quickly; but not before she had grabbed Anna by the arm. Taking Ellie by the scruff, she quieted as I led her into the garage. Back to Anna, who was traumatized and in pain; I was still outside of myself, doing what was needed at the moment but feeling no emotion. Ellie had broken skin, had bitten our friend. *She's dead,* I thought to myself. *Chris is going to kill her. Why? Why? Why, Ellie?* Without emotion, I observed my thoughts. Anna, crying and relating a story of being attacked by a large dog as a child. Her screams as Ellie charged toward her, elevating the dog even more. Reacting with the childhood memory charging her, she had cried out to me, "Cindi! Help me! Cindi!" Now, back in the house, we looked at her wounds. I switched into nurse mode, cleaning the physical damage, and soothing the emotional harm. It wasn't until several minutes later when I went out to Ellie in the garage that I came fully back into myself and burst into tears. "Ellie! Why, Ellie? You just bought your way to heaven, Ellie! Why did you do that?! Anna is our friend, and you know that!" My tears spilled over Ellie's head and muzzle. She wagged her tail slowly and buried her head into my chest. "Why are you here, Ellie. Why is this dog in my life?"

All of us were being prepared for difficult lessons, and our guides and angels had been sending signals continuously. Anna delayed by one thing after another trying to leave Minneapolis to join us in a tiny Wisconsin town for a weekend of what we expected was going to be meditation with a Buddhist Lama. First coming home to her dog having been sick on their white carpets in three rooms. Then, in the comically slowest line at the grocery store for items to clean the carpets. Then, back to the store after realizing she had forgotten to purchase the vegetables she needed for the weekend's potluck lunches. More still, as she finally headed east only to find the highway exit to Highway 94 toward Hudson closed. So many messages delivered!

Almost a two-hour drive from our home, Chris and I arrived for the Friday evening talk a few minutes late. The friend who had invited us to the weekend gathering was not there, called away to help a family member. The atmosphere was not nearly as elevated as we had anticipated. The Tibetan Lama's English was difficult to follow; his presentation voice monotonous as he addressed the small group. I forget now what his message that evening was. Anna arrived for the last twenty minutes of the evening, and the three of us drove together back to Chris's and my home.

Pulling into the garage after the long drive, gathering up our bags, books, and Anna's luggage, Chris tried to grab just one more bag. A mason jar crashed to the painted concrete, shattering into countless fragments, glass shards covering the garage floor. Another message.

As I walked the dogs under the stars, fatigue set in. I was exhausted. Back inside, Ellie kenneled and upset that there was someone other than us in her house. Ellie knew Anna, she and her husband had visited on several occasions. No matter, Ellie was upset. Another message. Dogs settled, the three of us chatted for a bit and then said good night.

Early the next morning, as we prepared for another long drive to the Lama, a framed photo collage of Chris's family flew off of the bookshelf; glass frame shattering in pieces on the dining room floor. *What the?!* None of us, nor the dogs, were near the shelf when the picture took flight. Rushing to clean up the mess before dog paws could be injured, the energy of the day was now infused with stress and chaos.

We again arrived late for the day with the Lama. His droning voice was quickly lulling me into boredom. *Why am I here?* Seven hours later, as he ended the day saying something about wasting time, the A-HA hit me. *THIS is wasting my time. We are not supposed to be here.* Our friend had been missing again today. Perhaps she would have made the experience something other than what we were living. Chris and I were having the same thoughts. We are not coming back here tomorrow for another day of this. Anna had just had a private meeting with the Lama. How to tell her we weren't coming back...

We did not go back for the final day with the small group. And now I was experiencing the grief and guilt that this was all my fault, that Ellie would in all likelihood be dead in less than a day's time. "What's wrong? You look like someone just died." Chris asked as he joined us in the living room following his morning meditation. Tears again spilled as I explained what had happened, that it was entirely my fault, that Ellie had just charged Anna.

"You're going to kill her, aren't you?" I asked. Now Anna is spilling tears and distraught, "No, no, no!" she exclaimed. "Ellie is who she is, was just being who she is. I startled her. Please don't put her down because of me. I will be fine. This was my fault. I screamed. I shouldn't have screamed."

Chris was angry, livid that Ellie had harmed our dear friend. "She attacked a person. She has to go."

Back in the garage, Ellie wagging her tail and having returned to her usual, happy self. I sat with her, replaying the entire scene in my mind. The truth was painful. It was me; I was still Ellie's problem. *It's YOU. You are Ellie's problem*. The very moment I had heard Anna's greeting, "Hi, Cindi!" I was triggered and disassociated. Ellie, responding on my behalf, being triggered and flipping backward in time, she started fighting. She didn't know *what* she was fighting. Triggered and sent back in time, fighting, trying to be alive.

Why was this happening? Why was I sitting in a cold garage with a dog I couldn't help? *Because Ellie doesn't need help, you do. YOU are Ellie's problem. You must heal yourself if you are to help Ellie.* For the third time in Ellie's life, I asked, to myself this time, "What happens to her now?"

It's too late, I thought. She will be euthanized in the morning. This time no one was kidding. This time it was real. I turned my back on Ellie, my heart broken, shattered with love for this dog; and returned to the house. Anna insisted that Ellie not be put down because of this incident. Chris's anger mellowed, and he agreed. Ellie would be kept on leash, and I would work through my trapped emotions. Emotions that were causing me to trigger Ellie; keeping both of us from forward progress.

Ellie never harmed another human. She and I worked diligently on releasing our triggers. Me working tirelessly on socializing Ellie, on discovering what in the environment was triggering *me* which then triggered *her*. Have I discovered them all, all of our triggers? How can I know? I can't know. I can, however, continue on this journey with Ellie, showing her that her world is safe, being vigilant in keeping her present and safe without the need to ever flip backward in time again.

FIVE WINTERS

Ellie's journey has been measured in winters, maybe because it is the time of year she loves most. Watching Ellie lope through fields of untracked new-fallen snow is a thing of breathtaking beauty; her thick coat and strong body were made for just this, following in the pawprints of her St. Bernard ancestors, the Hospice Dogs of old.

Ellie's fifth winter was marked by many forward steps on her path toward healing. She is more accepting, even relaxed, when we have visitors in our home. The work she and I are doing; me continually telling her that only good people will be near her, that, "Everyone is a friend, Ellie," is now sinking in. Ellie and Olive are best friends, and Olive no longer lives in hiding; secluded in my loft office. Years have passed since Ellie has shown any aggression toward Olive.

Ellie's fear of water is receding. When Ellie needs a bath, she willingly, although perhaps not enthusiastically, steps into the bathtub when I ask her to; a good thing as I cannot budge her if she chooses to say, Thanks, but NO, I'd rather keep this dirt on me. And, over the previous summer and autumn, Ellie ventured down to the lake and put a toe in the water. Standing on a floating bog at the very edge of the shore, she took a drink of lake water; front paws sinking as Ellie's weight caused her perch to dip slightly. Ellie did not panic. Instead, allowed her legs to submerge a few inches as she lapped up the refreshing water.

Ellie discovered that the spruce bog is a fun place to run when there is not snow covering it. She raced and ran and teased Olive to join her, leaping and bounding and turning tight corners around the small, ancient trees. There is peace in this place that visitors can feel. "You live in a magical place," a friend mused after seeing a photograph of our land at the peak of fall's brilliance. Yes, we live in a magical place. We have done much work to fill our forest, bog, lake, and home with the energy of peace and love. It is a palpable feeling to enter this space. It has been Ellie's healing place. It has been my healing place.

Our journey of healing Ellie will continue for as long as she walks with us in this life. Her willingness to let go and move forward has revealed so much. Ellie's healing journey has been a great gift to me, though at times my heart burned with pain and doubt. Sometimes we need to hold our hearts over that burning fire to fully witness alchemy. Alchemy within ourselves and those we love; the dogs, the humans, all sentient beings. *I've watched your alchemical process, Ellie, watched as you have transformed yourself through your rage to great big love. You are a great big love, Ellie. I love you.*

Healing Ellie, Healing Me has been a remarkable journey that I will carry with me for all time; perhaps the lessons will come a little easier in another life. Today, I am simply grateful.

Epilogue

Another winter morning, clear sky and very, very cold. Guidance suggested I walk Kato and Olive on leash on the road instead of our usual romp on the frozen lake. Having learned the lesson not to ignore my higher self, and although Kato would have much preferred a high-energy game of snow Frisbee, I attached leashes, and we walked the forested roads.

I am clairaudient. My greatest intuitive strength, I hear with my mind's eye. Not words such as these on a written page or voice, but instead a flood of information received all at once in the form of energy buzzing in my ears. Now, walking quietly with Olive and Kato both ears were ringing, each with a different frequency of vibration, and I heard a great truth. Something had been bothering me. *What is it? What is going on with the dogs? So many of the dogs? Why is Dog suffering?* The answer poured into my awareness:

They are responding. You say it yourself in your work often, 'Our dogs respond to who we are, to how we show up in the world.' They are responding. Responding to humanity. To how humans treat one another and how they treat themselves. Yes, there have always been, and perhaps will continue to be, wars among peoples. Violence, hatred, unspeakable acts of torture and cruelty in all corners of the planet. Today much of humanity witnesses all of this atrocity via your technology. The dogs of your childhood are a mere memory. Dog is evolving just as Humanity is evolving; some rising up, some sinking to great depths, others trapped on a plane of despondent lethargy. Yes, there are still many good dogs, just as there are still many good people. But Dog is suffering, just as Humanity is suffering, just as Earth is suffering, just as all on Earth are suffering. You know this in your heart to be truth. You must continue to open your heart and help. Help fix it. With love. Only love can fix it. Work hard and work fast. Be deliberate. Don't hurry.

I take this message, this gift from guidance to heart. It is my intention in my work and in all that I do to bring light and healing to all; to all dogs, to all people, to all living beings, with love.

~ Namaste

Cindi with Labrador Kato

Animal Communicator, Canine Behavior Consultant, and Intuitive Healer; Cindi McGrath has devoted her life's work to the Dog. From the age of two, there has always been a dog, or many dogs, at Cindi's side. As a young adult, Cindi raised and showed Boxer dogs in the Confirmation ring; trained a spirited young Labrador in the sport of Agility; and, more recently has shared many life lessons with a beautiful Rottweiler, three Labradors, and Ellie, a very large St. Bernard-Great Dane mix. In 2011 she left a successful career in business to follow her passion of working with animals. With her husband Chris and their dogs, Cindi lives in Northwest Wisconsin surrounded by the woods, water, and wildlife of the Chequamegon National Forest. She can be reached at www.ThisWayCanines.org

Quick Order Form

Healing Ellie Healing Me **$16.95** plus Shipping

Website: **www.Inpspire-Ink.com**

Email: info@Inspire-Ink.com
ThisWayCanines@gmail.com

Postal Orders:
Inspire Ink
This Way! Canines
P.O. Box 874
Hayward, WI 54843

Name:_____

Address:_____

City:_____ State:_____ Zip:_____

Telephone:_____

Email Address:_____

Sales Tax: Please add 5.5% for books shipped to
Wisconsin addresses.

Shipping:
United States $3.00 for the first book and $2.00 for each
additional book.
International $9.00 for the first book and $5.00 for each
additional book.